The Role of Montessori in Educating
Children of this Generation *and* Beyond

Books by the author

THE ECONOMICS OF EDUCATION AND THE
FUTURE OF SOCIETIES

ENGLISH GRAMMAR: A TEACHING GUIDE
FOR ELEMENTARY AND ADVANCED
LEARNERS OF ENGLISH

HOW THE INTERNET CAN TAKE YOUR KIDS
OUT OF POVERTY: 10 RULES TO CHANGE
YOUR CHILDREN'S DESTINY

SURVIVING IN THE SEMINARY

THE DEATH OF EDUCATION

*T*he Role of Montessori in Educating Children of this Generation and Beyond

ALLAN H. AMOGUIS

SAVVY PUBLISHING COMPANY

Book and Cover Designs: Bernard Fababaer

First Edition

ISBN 97-88-8902396-2-5

Printed in Italy by SPC Publishing
Via Virano 119, Veroli, 03029 Frosinone

This author wishes to express his deep
appreciation to Prof. *Raniero Regni,*
Lumsa University, Rome, Italy
for his moral support.

TABLE OF CONTENTS

ACKNOWLEDGEMENT

I would like to thank, above all, the Creator of Heaven and Earth for having given me the possibility to be in the world today, where His love reigns in every single creature of which human beings, to whom the plan of salvation in the spiritual domain has been revealed, have been entrusted with the mission to proclaim the Gospel to all; in a special way, an expression of gratitude goes to two of these persons, Allaine Maria Jeena and Dominic Savio, for without their hardwork in bringing to completion the proofreading task, the pages of this book would not have been put together with sense and accuracy. They have done an enormous sacrifice in rendering this work, difficult and challenging in all its aspects, to a readable and comprehensible form.

Saint Paul the Apostle, from whom I get much inspiration to carry out the Christian mission, said:

"He will keep you steadfast to the end, and you will be without reproach on the day of the coming of our Lord Jesus."[1] (I Corinthians 1:8).

1   *Christian Community Bible*, Ed, Bernardo Hurault (China: Nanjing Amity Pinting Company, 2003), p. 332.

PREFACE

The author of this work has imposed upon himself the obligation of presenting in a formal way – using the qualitative research methodology through systematic surveys of authors in the field – the scientific findings of Angeline Stoll Lillard, who authored the book, *MONTESSORI: The Science Behind The Genius* (2005) on the role of peer learning (present in Montessori schools) in education today. The present endeavor, which by no means claims to be the sole introductory work on the subject, has been written in support of the Lillardian scholarly findings on this issue.

Over the past decades, many studies have been conducted – all with the aim in mind of improving educational systems in general, and focusing on the approaches to teaching children in particular. These approaches, most often than not, have strengthened the importance of child-centered education to this effect. Kathryn H. Au and Jacquelin H. Carroll, in their article, *Current Research on Classroom Instruction: Goals, Teachers' Actions, and Assessment,* said that:

"New ideas about classroom instruction are perhaps best understood against the backdrop of the paradigm shift taking place in educational psychology, as research perspectives have changed from behaviorism to cognitive science to social constructivism. In the behaviorist and cognitive science perspectives, instruction is seen as a process of transmission from teacher to student, and the guiding metaphor is that of the conduit. In the conduit metaphor, the teacher sends or transmits a signal that is received by the student. The signals are unidirectional, implying that instruction is monologic."[2]

Now comes one pretty clear message from this pronouncement: the changing role of a teacher from an all-knowing transmitter rendering, as it were, the whole and traditionalistic instructional processes *monologic*, to a more student-centered, pragmatic and constructivist approach to learning.[3] This, indeed, has become a more urgent discussion for educators to focus on than ever before, and as Janet Moyles noted:

> "There is confusion at every level as to what is appropriate pedagogical practice [...]."[4]

Peer learning has really been but a well-supported alternative solution to the present school system, which has long been crumbling

2 Deborah L Speech and Keogh, Barbara K. Keogh, eds, *Research on Classroom Ecologies: Implications for Inclusion of Children With Learning Disabilities,* in Kathryn H. Au and Jacquelin H. Carroll, *Current Research on Classroom Instruction: Goals, Teachers' Actions, and Assessment* (New Jersey: Lawrence Erlbaum Associates, Publishers, 1996), p. 17.
3 Nancy Falchikov, *Learning Together: Peer Tutoring in Higher Education.* London: RoutledgeFalmer, 2001), p. 67.
4 J. R. Moyles, *Organizing for Learning in the Primary Classroom: A Balanced Approach to Classroom Management* (Philadelphia: Open University Press., 1992), p.13.

away desperately into the depth of ineffectiveness. Talking on behalf of American schools, Mary Bay wrote:

"A major impetus for the attention has been the national discourse on the *failure* of our nation's schools to educate all of our students at challenging levels."[5]

This *failure* to educate necessitates a new paradigm to education, a new way of understanding how education really works and what it intends to achieve in the long run. What it intended to be in the past could have been a historically obsolete way of judging how this generation understands it to be, as Doris Pronin clearly stated:

"In the United States, early childhood education, the education of children from birth to 9 years, grew out of Western European traditions during the 19th century and evolved through the 1950s out of a maturationist,

5   Bernie Y. L Wong. and Mavis L. Donahue, Eds., *The Social Dimensions of Learning Disabilities: Essays in Honor of Tanis Bryan*, in Mary Bay, *Preparing Prospective Teachers to Work in the Social and Emotional Worlds of Students With Learning Disabilities* (New Jersey: Lawrence Erlbaum Associates, Publishers, 2002), p.115.

linear child development framework that still predominates. This linear framework, laced with a strong measure of sentiment and caring, meshes with the predominant public elementary school image of learning as discrete additive steps and stages. Within this academic framework, education focuses on the attainment of universal skills and a body of information. In the pursuit of these goals, in the name of developing a citizenry capable of democratic governance and a competent workforce, elementary education policy-makers have set a priority on the development of reading, writing, and arithmetic skills. Most schools have shared these goals and made the three Rs the centerpiece of primary education."[6]

What is indeed predominant in the present educational system on a worldwide scale is this focus on the attainment of universal skills and a body of information – all in the name of developing a citizenry capable of democratic governance and a competent workforce. To personalize professional learning may well

---

6   Bruce Torff and Robert J. Sternberg, Eds., *Understanding and Teaching the Intuitive Mind: Student and Teacher Learning*, in Doris Pronin, *The Intuitive Mind and Early Childhood Education: Connections with Chaos Theory, Script Theory, and Theory of Mind* (New Jersey: Lawrence Erlbaum Associates, Publishers, 2001), p. 93.

be the key to change the situation for the better.[7] Pronin's conclusion couldn't have been more apt to describe this horror:

> "In my opinion, this sort of linear, world-to-child schooling in early childhood is a form of sanctioned child abuse."[8]

Frosinone,
August 2016

ALLAN H. AMOGUIS

---

7   Pam Robbins, *Peer Coaching: To Enrich Professional Practice, School Culture, and Student Learning* (Virginia: ASCD, 2015), p. 9.
8   Ibid.

INTRODUCTION

Our present school system has stopped working since time immemorial. Maria Montessori's educational method comes at the moment when today's pedagogists and scientists are on the run looking for the best alternative to compensate, if not totally replace, the current system. The ironical part to take note of here, however, is the fact that the alternative that educators have been longing to discover – ways in which to fix the system – has been available since the nineteenth century, for, as it turned out to be, the world ignored the relevance of the method back then for its seemingly anachronistic way of viewing the world and of conceiving an educational system that is far away from the intellectual capability of the mainstream society at that time to assimilate and accommodate it.

The obsolete idea of having our children come to school to listen to a teacher talk for very long hours has been too much for us to bear. This whole system can be replaced by the revolutionary idea of peer learning (as one of the best alternatives we have so far). By having children learn by themselves, and for themselves, we undoubtedly present them with the most natural way of discovering this planet (and everything around it), an essential evolutionary process especially relevant for our species to move forward. With this in mind, the role of Maria Montessori in educating children of this generation and beyond comes into the scene!

It is therefore the aim of this author – through the studies undertaken by Dr. Angeline Lillard and scholars in the field – to give a convincing proposition to the merits of Peer Learning (embodied fully in any Montessori learning environment) as a substitute educative approach which is capable of impacting both the child's cognitive and social developments.

Although the terms peer, collaborative, and cooperative are not solely attributable to Montessori methods of learning as a whole, this author would examine, specifically, the cognitive and social aspects of peer learning as embodied in Maria Montessori's approach to education.

1 PEER LEARNING: MEANING AND COMMON UNDERSTANDING

Peer Learning as it stands has more to it than it sounds; it means so many things to different types of educators, with each meaning not to be obviously disparaged for whatever discriminating reasons there may be. David Boud and his colleagues present the following definition as a bird's-eye view to the concept:

> "Peer learning is not a single, un-differentiated educational strategy. It encompasses a broad sweep of activities. For example, researchers from the University of Ulster identified 10 different models of peer learning. These ranged from the traditional proctor model, in which senior students tutor junior students, to the more innovative learning cells, in which students in the same year form partnerships to assist each other with both course content and personal concerns. Other models involved discussion seminars, private study groups, *parrainage* (a buddy system) or counseling, peer-

assessment schemes, collaborative project or laboratory work, projects in different sized (cascading) groups, workplace mentoring and community activities."[9]

William Damon provides a more systematic understanding of this approach, which this author uses as a starting point for this work, when he said:

> "[...] Two different forms of peer learning, "peer tutoring" and "peer collaboration," are distinguished. Each has its potential use: peer tutoring for transmitting information and drilling special skills; peer collaboration for facilitating intellectual discovery and the acquisition of basic knowledge."[10]

Peer tutoring and peer collaboration, as defined by Damon, characterize peer learning both in terms of information transmission and facility in acquiring knowledge. Both these definitions fit in the concept of peer learning to

9 David Boud, Ruth Cohen, and Jane Sampson, Eds., *Peer Learning in Higher Education: Learning from & with each other* (Virginia: Stylus Publishing Inc., 2001). p.3.
10 William Damon, *"Peer Education: The Untapped Potential,"* Journal of Applied Developmental Psychology 5 (October 1984), p. 331.

be two-directional, as opposed to a unidirectional approach in the traditional sense. In a more specific context, "[…] Peer tutoring is an approach in which one child instructs another child in material on which the first is an expert and the second a novice."[11]

The distinction, however, between the two functions of peer learning – although understood here specifically to be an act of *transmitting* and *facilitating* in its core meaning – is nonetheless far from being objectively conclusive. The variations to the aforementioned definitions would all depend upon the context in which learning takes place. David Boud and his colleagues clarified:

> "The term 'peer learning', however, remains abstract. The sense in which we use it here suggests a two-way, reciprocal learning activity. Peer learning should be mutually beneficial and involve the sharing of knowledge, ideas and experience between the participants. It can be described as a way of

11 William Damon and Erin Phelps, in *Critical Distinctions Among Three Approaches To Peer Education*, Journal of Applied Developmental Psychology (October 1984): Vol. 13, p. 11.

moving beyond independent to *interdependent* or mutual learning [...]."[12]

The expert to novice idea which implies the traditional concept of tutoring, as best exemplified in the present school system, plays an important role in understanding the second defining implication – the precise comprehension of which far exceeds the importance of the first signification – as it involves, as it were, this concept of interdependence, a child helping another child in discovering and exploring the world and its complexities with one child having a little advanced knowledge over the other and thus serving as a peer support. Tony Charlton and Kevin Jones, in their article, *Peer support practices in classrooms and schools,* explained that:

> "By 'peer support' we refer to those instances (usually planned and under the supervision or guidance of a teacher) where pupils are directly involved in organizing and delivering experiences to help maximize some aspect of their peers' functioning (i.e their affective, social, physical and cognitive performance). [...] While peer support is

---

12 D. Boud, et. al., p.3.

usually offered to pupils of the same age, it can be offered also to younger ones (cross-age support)."[13]

Peer learning under this present study – limiting a definition though it may be – will be understood here in terms of its transmitting and facilitating functions, with emphasis on the role of educators as being facilitators wherein learning is undertaken by the children themselves. What happens in the actual learning environment must be understood as a product of the children's natural way of acquiring knowledge based more on their individual thirst for discovery about anything nature could offer them than the skills-acquisition method imposed upon them by educational systems of governments.

---

13 Kevin Jones and Charlton, Tony Charlton, Eds., *Overcoming Learning and Behaviour Difficulties: Partnership with Pupils*, in Tony Charlton and Kevin Jones, *Peer support practices in classrooms and schools* (New York: Routledge, 1996), p. 92.

1.1   ANGELINE LILLARD'S THREE FORMS OF PEER LEARNING

The methods of Maria Montessori, in the context of peer learning as they have been applied in Montessori schools, will be thoroughly dealt with in terms of – but not limited to – the definitions given in the preceding paragraphs. Angeline Lillard's exposition of the method and how she discovered the science behind this approach will be treated here as a principal theoretical framework of the book, arguing on the basis of her three forms of learning from and with peers: 1) Learning from peers by observation and imitation; 2) Peer tutoring and 3) Collaborative learning. Lillard commented:

> "In this chapter I discuss three forms of learning from and with peers in terms of research on those forms and their presence in Montessori education. The first, learning

from peers by observation and imitation, is rarely implemented in traditional schools, as will be discussed. The second, peer tutoring, is being used increasingly. In such arrangements, peers help each other in the learning process, rather than working as competing autonomous units [...]. The third form is collaborative learning, or learning interactively among people of fairly similar ability levels, and it is also being implemented with increasing frequency in traditional classrooms."[14]

Although not fully given equal attention due to the scope and limitation of this study, the discussion on collaborative learning will be treated fairly but briefly. Studies on Collaborative Learning, Team Learning, and the like, have been in themselves big branches of research on this field.

---

14 Angeline Stoll Lillard, *Montessori: The Science Behind The Genius (New York: Oxford University Press, 2005)*, p. 195. Chapter 6 of this book has the title: *Learning from Peers*.

1.2 DEEPER MEANING OF PEER LEARNING

On a profound level, peer learning (or learning in general) should be able to bring about a positive change both in an individual and in society for it to be considered wholly efficacious and effective. Norman Miller and Jordan Harrington, in their article, *A Situational Identity Perspective on Cultural Diversity and Teamwork in the Classroom,* stated that:

> "A fundamental question for educational instruction is: What is the most important thing for schools to teach students (or for students to learn in school)? In response, Johnson and Johnson (1978) state that it is 'how to build and maintain positive relationships with other people.' They argue that cooperation is the cornerstone to building and maintaining 'stable families, career success, neighborhood and community membership, important values and beliefs, friendships, and contributions to society' and conclude that 'there is no aspect of human experience more basic and important than

cooperating with others.'"[15]

One of the defining arguments of this scholastic work, therefore, lies in the outcome and goal of learning and what it could contribute to the well-being of an individual, as well as what it can offer to the progress of society in which that same individual resides. Peer learning, as this author would argue, plays an important role to the realization of this goal. Miller and Harrington wrote:

> "Children with poor peer adjustment are at risk for later difficulty in life."[16]

---

15 Shlomo Sharan, Ed., *COOPERATIVE LEARNING: Theory and Research*, In Norman Miller and Hugh Jordan Harrington, *A Situational Identity Perspective on Cultural Diversity and Teamwork in the Classroom* (Connecticut London: Praeger Westport, 1990). p. 11
16 Ibid., p.39.

2 PEER LEARNING IN MARIA MONTESSORI'S EDUCATIVE APPROACH

The majority of schools across the globe today – due, in fact, to this long history of a militaristic form of education, a living legacy of a system patterned according to the styles of the Victorian Era – are quite aware that peer learning happens rarely, if at all; in contrast, in Montessori schools peer learning is understood to be a daily and commonplace event inside a classroom. Lillard reported that:

"In traditional elementary school classrooms, children learn mainly from the teacher and texts. The teacher stands before the children, who are seated at individual desks, and delivers knowledge. Elementary school classrooms are engaged in this form of instruction (on average) 60-70% of the time, with much of the rest of the time spent in individual seat work and transitioning; the percentage of time spent in lectures is thought to increase in high school [...]."[17]

When children sit most of the time inside a classroom where all they are expected to do is listen to the teacher, what happens is a unidirectional form of interaction – and with this long hours of sitting together doing clerical work, children naturally begin to fidget.[18] Lillard has precisely noted the fact that traditional teachers do stand in front of children and deliver knowledge – either consciously or otherwise, an act which Doris Pronin, as earlier mentioned, termed as 'sanctioned child abuse' (especially when teachers load the children with a body of information in doing so).

Maria Montessori's method is a deconstruction of this traditional form of education. Peer learning, in its most constructivist form, has been valued as one of the best available educational alternatives to traditional schooling. Angeline Lillard wrote:

---

17 Lillard, p. 192.
18 Robinson, K. (2013, May). *Ken Robinson: How to escape education's death valley* [Video file]. Retrieved from https://www.youtube.com/watch?v=wX78iKhInsc. Proper mention began at 05.30'.

"In contrast, peer learning is embedded in the structure of Montessori education. Children are free to work together and they often do, particularly as they get older and more socially inclined. Self-formed groups of two or more children might work together on maps or math problems or reports. Yet Dr. Montessori noted that others often criticized her schools as asocial, because of the lack of whole-class, uniform activity."[19]

On one hand, this freedom to work together in pursuit of knowledge while discovering the world around them is an innate characteristic of children; on the other hand, contrary to common belief that Montessori schools are (as seen by critics) asocial – arguing in favor of the context of traditional schools having this communistic mass-grouping system where children are huddled together apparently to be instructed. Quoting Dr. Maria Montessori, Lillard said:

"Teachers who use direct methods cannot understand how social behavior is fostered in a Montessori school. They think it

---

19 Lillard, 193.

offers scholastic material but not social material. They say, "If the child does everything on his own, what becomes of social life?" But what is social life if not the solving of social problems, behaving properly and pursuing aims acceptable to all? [It is not] sitting side by side and hearing someone else talk. [...]

The only social life that children get in the ordinary schools is during playtime or on excursions. Ours live always in an active community."[20]

In this context, what is pretty obvious is the fact that – understanding it from the perspective of common and logical sense – putting the children together to listen to a teacher for hours and hours on end is in itself not a social activity on the part of the children. And that's exactly where the problem lies. John Biggs explained:

"Learning takes place through the active behavior of the student: it is what *he* does that he learns, not what the teacher does. - Ralph W. Tyler (1949)."[21]

20 Ibid., p.194.
21 J. Biggs, *Teaching for Quality Learning at University: What the Student Does* (United Kingdom: McGraw-Hill House, 2003), p. V.

The method of Maria Montessori does exactly that. The child is the protagonist of the learning process, actively involved in it most of the time during the school hours. Discussing her method on the significance of a child learning from another child, Dr. Montessori wrote:

> "Our schools show that children of different ages help one another. The younger ones see what the older ones are doing and ask for explanations. These are readily given, and the instruction is really valuable, for the mind of a five year old is so much nearer than ours to the mind of a child of three...The older ones are happy to be able to teach what they know. There are no inferiority complexes, but everyone achieves a healthy normality through the mutual exchange. – Maria Montessori [...]."[22]

A child can more effectively relate to another child than to an adult. On one hand, the problem of 'generation gap' is resolved; on the other hand, the use of language between the two to explain concepts and ideas is far more common than what it would have been with a

_____
22   Ibid., p. 192.

much older person. Jean H. Guilmette and Maureen O'Neil wrote:

"Our experience has proven that [peer learning] is an efficient way to transmit knowledge across a wide range of groups or regions. Peer learning, based on jointly generated evidence, is also an effective means to build capacity and foster scientific excellence. The body of knowledge it generates is a powerful tool for the development of evidence-based policy."[23]

In fact, Montessori's method – which itself had withstood the test of time – has been building capacity and fostering scientific excellence in children across the continents. The child, an active discoverer of this method, is the active participant of the learning process. Lillard wrote:

"Underlying Montessori education is a model of the child as a motivated doer rather than an empty vessel. The active child is a view often credited to Jean Piaget, who may

23 Jean H. Guilmette and Maureen O'Neil, *Power of Peer Learning : Networks and Development Cooperation* (Ottawa: International Development Research Centre, 2009), p. v. Foreword to their work.

have been influenced by Dr. Montessori. [...]"[24]

2.1 LEARNING THROUGH OBSERVATION AND IMITATION

Observation and *imitation* are two significant key words of the Montessori method. The act of observing, as well as the act of imitating, comes with a thorough educative implication. Observing and imitating both serve as backbones to learning activities as a whole. Peers learn from one another by observing what the other is doing, and then – as a natural consequence of this act – this observation would bring the observing child to imitate (or copy) what he or she has observed into his or her own reality, as Lillard has pointed out:

> "Clearly all people learn in part by observing and imitating others [...]. Yet the importance of imitative learning was not

---

24 Lillard, p. 28. Talking about Jean Piaget and Dr. Montessori on this paragraph, Lillard continued: "[…] He was 26 years her junior and early in his career had conducted observations for his book *The Language and Thought of the Child* in a Montessori school. He apparently attended at least one Montessori conference, in Rome in 1934, and was president of the Swiss Montessori Society.[...]"

highlighted in psychology and education during the heyday of behaviorism in the first half of the 20th century. In the early 1960s, the psychologist Albert Bandura provided the classic evidence that learning can occur through observation and imitation [...]."[25]

While educators around the world have been searching for alternative ways to learning, Dr. Maria Montessori – a visionary whose ideas were definitely much ahead of her time – discovered early on that children learn by observing and imitating, a legacy which brings about a clear sign for her "capacity to see facts, recording and interpreting them in order to understand the needs of children in their way to construct knowledge from the environment. [...] this is the fruit of her timely and indefatigable observation – herself never ever satisfied with the amount of work she put in – that unites scientific knowledge and imagination. [...]"[26]

25 Ibid., 195.
26 Paola Trabalzini (a cura di), "Maria Montessori Diario di una scienziata: imparare osservando," VITA DELL'INFANZIA Anno LXIII, N. 1e 2 (Settembre/Ottobre, 2014): 31. This is my personal translation from the orginal Italian text.

Learning by observing and imitating, as Dr. Montessori envisioned it, holds the answer to most of the riddles and dilemmas confronting educators and scientists in this generation; it would serve as the principal engine that would revolutionize, if applied on a greater scale, the present educational system from one that has stopped functioning to the true nature of how children should learn. Lillard explained:

"Traditional schooling capitalizes very little on this ubiquitous form of learning. In traditional arrangements, children may learn how to sit still at their desks and answer questions by observing others doing so, and perhaps might gain some insight into the thought processes of others when hearing them answer a question out loud. But because most learning in traditional schools occurs by transmission from teacher or texts to student, and then within each student as he or she works out problems alone, very little of the learning process is available for others to absorb through observation and imitation. In Montessori, as will be seen, learning by observation and imitation happens easily and naturally [...]"[27]

Experimental findings on observational learning support the Montessori method. Another surprising finding, said Lillard, regarding observation and imitation is how effective (at any age) even almost subliminal modeling can be. "If a person sees someone else engage in such behaviors as yawning, scratching their nose, or shaking their foot, the observing person is quite likely to engage in that same behavior [...]."[28]

Angeline Lillard further said: "In one study, toddlers were shown how a special stick could be used in a particular way to retrieve an object from a tube [...]. Even 2-year-olds could repeat the precise actions necessary to retrieve the object, showing that toddlers can learn to use tools in very particular ways via observation and imitation."[29]

The Montessori method uses observation and imitation with an aim of being able to

---

27 Lillard, pp.195-196.
28 Ibid., 196.
29 Ibid.

undertake the task as natural as possible, letting the kids discover by themselves what the prepared environment (for Montessori classrooms are organized and arranged before children would come in the room) could offer them. Lillard wrote:

> "The hands-on nature of Montessori work enables learning by observation and imitation. With Montessori materials, the abstract is made concrete, and (as the theory goes) by manipulating the concrete objects in particular ways, the abstract concepts are discovered by children. All that children have to learn via their observations, then, is the steps one takes with the concrete materials, which are easily visible [...]"[30]

---

30 Ibid., p.197.

2.2   PEER TUTORING

What peer tutoring does effectively would be the rightful turning over to Mother Nature the task of transmitting knowledge and drilling special skills to students by way of letting the seekers of knowledge learn them purposefully from a peer, a companion not distant from his or her own age and well within his or her intellectual reach – as opposed to the traditional learning method where teachers bombard children with information that they are not particularly interested in or are not psychologically and mentally willing to learn about. In the article, **Paired Learning in Literacy**, Keith Topping reported that:

> "Reviews of research on peer tutoring consistently find that structured methods of tutoring are associated with better measured outcomes. [...] They aim to efficiently scaffold the interactive learning process and also enable student self-management of learning and the

development of greater meta-cognitive awareness. [...] These methods are Paired Reading, Cued Spelling, and Paired Writing."[31]

Dedicated research and valuable scientific evidence (focusing especially on expert-novice studies) have strongly shown positive results on the role of peer tutoring in improving and giving education its real meaning.[32] Dennie Briggs said:

> "Contrary to popular belief, most of the world's children learn the basic skills of communication and survival from one another. Older children pass on the shortcuts they've learned by trial-and-error to their juniors along with those aspects of their culture that they have found useful to become more independent: elementary things like how to put on your clothes, what to avoid, how to manipulate adults."[33]

31 Keith Topping and Stewart Ehly, Eds., (1998). *Peer-Assisted Learning*, In Keith Topping, *Paired Learning in Literacy* (New Jersey: Lawrence Erlbaum Associates, 1998), p. 87.
32 Joseph Psotka, Dan L. Massey, et al., *Intelligent Tutoring Systems: Lessons Learned*. In Barbara Means, *Cognitive Task Analysis as a Basis for Tutor Development: Articulating Abstract Knowledge Representations* (New Jersey: Lawrence Erlbaum Associates Publishers, 1998), p. 35.
33 Dennie Briggs, *A CLASS OF THEIR OWN: When Children Teach Children* (Connecticut: Greenwood Publishing Group, 1998), p. 1.

Moreover, peer tutoring has been impacting the lives of children on a social level. Ivan Frank wrote: "The American propensity to use mentors and tutors who become buddies to at-risk youth has begun to help youth in rural areas, as well as in the traditional urban programs. More than in the past, this has become an adjunct to peer group programs, and it has been very helpful."[34]

One important characteristic of the Montessori method lies in the fact that peer tutoring happens all the time. The activities set for the children are learning activities that the children themselves choose to know about, prompted by no one but their own curiosity. Lillard pointed this out as she said:

> "People learn more effectively from individualized instruction than from whole-class instruction [...]. Montessori education can capitalize on this because the teacher is free to work individually with children. The teacher can do so because the other children

---

34 Ivan C. Frank, *Building Self-Esteem in At-Risk Youth: Peer Group Programs and Individual Success Stories* (Connecticut: Praeger Westport, 1996), p. 1

are busy learning from the materials and each other. In traditional schooling, the teacher does not have time to tutor all the children individually, because school is not structured to have the remaining children work independently for most of the day. In addition to individual instruction from teachers, children can effectively tutor each other."[35]

The ability of a child to teach another child can never be underestimated. And "With ever-faster evolving technologies and pedagogical methods, there may, in fact, be areas where adults are less effective teachers than youngsters. [...]."[36] Given a proper environment, a child can release his or her potential and inherent gift for teaching. Lillard noted: "When tasks are appropriately structured, peers can be very effective tutors, and both tutor and tutee benefit academically and socially from the arrangement. [...]."[37]

When it comes to physical arrangement, Montessori schools are different. The concept of traditional structure where chairs and student

35 Lillard, p. 203.
36 Briggs, p. XIII. From the Foreword of his book.
37 Lillard, p. 204.

desks are facing the blackboard, and so on, has been considered unnatural in Montessori class structure. The Montessori environment, therefore, where peer tutoring can naturally occur – and where, obviously, children decide voluntarily on satisfying their own thirst for learning – is structured quite the opposite way traditional schools are structured. Judith W. Segal, and others, have said that:

> "Even in the earliest grades, teachers direct students to a lesson or reading assignment with instructions to learn information, concepts, or skills. Little is said to the child about how to go about learning. Recent research focused on reading has shown that explicit instruction in strategies for effective thinking and learning rarely occurs in classrooms [...]."[38]

Although the studies done above had its focus on reading, Lillard explained that "[...] a follow-up study expanded the peer tutoring to cover reading, math, and language, and

38 W. Segal, et al. , *Thinking and Learning Skills: Relating Instruction to Research* , Vol.1, In Susan F. Chipman and Judith W. Segal, *Higher Cognitive Goals for Education: An Introduction* (New Jersey: Lawrence Erlbaum Associated, 1985), p.1.

examined children's performance over multiple years. Children in the tutoring program performed significantly better than those in the control group on all three topics both immediately and two years later, when they had moved on to middle school and no longer had the program.[…]."[39]

Specific structures in peer tutoring have been advanced by both the Montessori methods of learning as well as the current studies on this regard. Lillard commented:

> "Peer tutoring programs vary in terms of how structured each tutoring session is, and more structured programs are typically associated with greater success. Reciprocal Peer Tutoring (RPT) is an example of a more structured tutoring program […], it has also been used to examine the effect of rewards. RPT begins with training sessions about teamwork and cooperation, and children are told they can win rewards by using teamwork. In the RPT program, teaching aides show the children how to tutor each other.[…]."[40]

---

39 Lillard, p. 204.
40 Ibid., 205.

Lillard explained one specific teaching strategy under the RPT, the Classwide Peer Tutoring: "One study of the efficacy of such a system (Classwide Peer Tutoring) involved first- and second-grade classrooms in low-income schools [...]. Classrooms were randomly assigned to tutoring and control conditions for spelling. In control classrooms, teachers used standard methods of teaching spelling: a workbook with word lists and vocabulary exercises, chalkboard, self-study, and home-work assignments. In classrooms that used the tutoring program, the tutoring process des-cribed earlier replaced some in-class spelling work. Over the two years of the study, children in the peer tutoring classrooms were spelling 87% of the words correctly on average, whereas children in other classrooms were spelling 75% of words correctly. This is an enormous difference, but it is certainly a meaningful one."[41]

In Montessori schools, however, it is a combination of what is understood to be both efficacious and effective in a child-centered

----

41 Ibid., p. 204.

learning environment. Lillard further explained that: "Peer tutoring occurs formally and informally in Montessori classrooms. Informally, younger children can learn from older ones in Montessori by asking them questions while watching them work. More formally, at the teacher's discretion, children in Montessori also sometimes show each other how to use a material.[...]."[42]

The freedom to interact with another student is one of the many significant characteristics of the Montessori method. The classroom is designed to provide this freedom. Lillard wrote:

"In sum, peer tutoring programs are beneficial to children even in traditional educational programs, where they are inserted as a break in the usual whole-class teaching day. In contrast, in Montessori education peer tutoring opportunities are built into the structure of the classroom. Children naturally learn from each other by asking, and teachers might ask children to show each other how to do a new work.

---

42 Ibid., p.209.

Tutees and tutors alike should benefit from such arrangements."[43]

2.3 COLLABORATIVE LEARNING

In a broader sense, peer tutoring is under the umbrella of collaborative learning. Lillard clarified it in her own words: "Whereas peer tutoring involves one student teaching another, collaborative learning refers to a group of two or more children working together. Several studies show that people learn better when working collaboratively than when working alone [...]."[44]

Elaborating on how collaboration works in Montessori environment, Lillard went on to say:

> "Many Montessori activities, especially at the Elementary level, can be done in pairs or small groups. Dr. Montessori noted this change in the orientation of the child at the second plane in her levels of development, as the child enters the Elementary classroom: 'A

---

43 Ibid., p. 210.
44 Ibid., p. 210.

third interesting fact to be observed in the child of six is his need to associate himself with others, not merely for the sake of company, but in some sort of organized activity. He likes to mix with others in a group wherein each has a different status' [...]."[45]

Collaborative learning translates into peer collaboration when "a pair of relative novices work together to solve challenging learning tasks that neither could do on their own prior to the collaborative engagement [...]"[46]

2.4 PEER LEARNING WITHIN MONTESSORI'S AGE-GROUPING

The question about the proper age for which peer learning can effectively be expected

---

45 Ibid., p. 215.
46 William Damon and Erin Phelps, "Critical Distinctions Among Three Approaches to Peer Education," International Journal of Educational Research, Vol.13 (1989), p.13. In relation to peer collaboration, the authors defined these terms further on the same page: "Unlike peer tutoring, the children begin at roughly the same levels of competence. Unlike cooperative learning, the learning at all times work jointly on the same problem rather than individually on separate components of the problem. This creates an engagement rich in mutual discovery, reciprocal feedback, and frequent sharing of ideas.[...]"

to yield maximum results in Montessori schools has been often asked of Montessori educators. Lillard said that "[...] The age of 6 is a pivotal one, recognized in many of the world's cultures as an appropriate time to ask more of children, such as by beginning formal schooling [...]. Six is the age at which Piaget speculated children advance to being able to perform mental operations (for example, imagining addition and subtraction), and which Dr. Montessori considered transitional between her first and second planes of development. [...]."[47]

In Dr. Maria Montessori's four planes of development, age 6 to 12 (which she calls Blue Plane of Childhood) is a period where children manifest an intense desire to learn and to argue, with that capacity of abstract thinking starting to develop from within their cognitive make-up – and "While the little child, with other children, could live and prosper in an atmosphere of unquestionable love, he would be able to build a social community [...]"[48]

47 Ibid., p. 207.
48 Camillo Grazzini, "Studi Montessori: I Quattro Piani dello Sviluppo," *Il Quaderno Montessori*, Anno XIII, numero 51 (Autunno 1996): 100-

While the age bracket from 6 to 12 is the ideal age for peer learning, Lillard pointed out that "Montessori encourages learning from peers in part by using three-year age groupings. [...] The multi-age groupings extend the possibility for learning by imitation, since children can learn from others who are just older. By viewing a 9- or even a 7-year-old at work, a 6-year-old can observe how the same material she uses to do a simpler mathematical procedure will be employed in progressively more complex ways as she gets older. Slightly older children might serve as the best kinds of models for learning to reenact structured sequences of action, from which much Montessori learning stems. [...]"[49]

Since there is no strict separation of classrooms in Montessori schools, children can freely go into another room where other children above or below their age are to be found.[50]

---

101. The four planes are: 0-6 ("Red Plane" of Infancy); 6-12 ("Blue Plane" of Childhood); 12-18 ("Red Plane" of Adolescence); 18-24 ("Blue Plane" of Maturity), pp. 100-103.

49 Lillard, p. 201.
50 Ibid., p. 202.

3   COGNITIVE ASPECTS OF PEER LEARNING

The psychology behind peer learning is rooted in its most fundamental and inherent principle in acquiring knowledge and skills. Jean Piaget's pioneering work in child development has been highly respected by scholars and scientists for more than half a century now. Richard De Lisi and Susan Golbeck wrote: "We find it helpful to segment the evolution of Piaget's theory into separate phases [...] and note that particularly in his early work (1920s-1930s), Piaget emphasized peer experiences as an important factor in child development."[51]

On a cognitive level, Angeline Lillard developed four key mechanisms which address the issue of why learning from peers is helpful:

---

51   A. M. O'Donnell and Alison King, Eds., *Cognitive Perspective on Peer Learning.* In Richard De Lisi and Susan Golbeck, *Implications of Piagetian Theory for Peer Learning* (p.3) (New Jersey: Lawrence Erlbaum Associates, Inc., 1999), p. 3.

incorporation, distributed cognition, active learning and motivation.[52]

3.1 INCORPORATION

According to Lillard, "One manner by which peers impact development is via imitation of others' behaviors and thought processes, which in due course may alter one's own cognitive structures. Piagetian and Vygotskian perspectives are compatible with this view. Clearly this sort of process occurs in observational learning. In one illustration of this, pairs of 5-year-olds were asked to recreate a Lego figure from a sample [...]. Experts behaved differently toward the model than novices, in that expert Lego builders looked a lot at the model. Novices benefited from being paired with an expert peer, but this was mediated by the extent to which they watched and imitated the expert.[...]"[53]

52 Lillard, p. 220.
53 Ibid.

Incorporation of a model into a child's cognitive processes is Lillard's way of explaining the vital role of Piaget's assimilation and accommodation concepts. In support of this, Dale H. Schunk wrote:

> "Modeling is an important means for acquiring skills, beliefs, attitudes, and behaviors [...]. Teachers, parents, and other adults serve as powerful models for children, but equally important are the many peers with whom children interact. Research shows that peer models play an important role in children's cognitive, social, and emotional development [...]."[54]

Modelling, Lillard stressed, is accomplished by way of observation and imitation. In elaborating this point, she explained: "Imitation studies have often involved adults as models, although the implication of the studies is clearly that children learn from all models, peer and adult alike. In fact, research has shown that young children learn from peer as well as adult models. In one study, an expert peer model

54 Keith Topping and Stewart Ehly, Eds., *Peer-Assisted Learning*, In Dale H. Schunk, *Peer Modelling* (New Jersey: Lawrence Erlbaum Associates, 1998), p. 185.

showed toddlers novel actions, and the toddlers imitated the actions two days later, even in different settings from those in which they had observed the model. [...]"[55]

As a cognitive aspect of peer learning, incorporation involves the child's natural ability to reproduce what his or her senses perceive and thereby acquire the knowledge and skills being offered on these common instances "[...] because children can incorporate a peer's behavior into their own repertoires. [...]."[56]

3.2 DISTRIBUTED COGNITION

Another cognitive aspect of peer learning is distributed cognition. Lillard supports the idea that "Distributed cognition is another explanation for why peer exchanges assist learning [...]. In collaboration, cognitive work is socially distributed, so the cognitive workload of each party is reduced. [...] people can talk back,

---

55 Lillard, p. 200.
56 Ibid., pp. 220-221.

exchange ideas, and fill in gaps in each other's knowledge, thereby raising the level of discussion. This can be especially important when each party brings skills or knowledge that another may lack, allowing different partners to serve as scaffolds for each other's learning. Peer tutoring exchanges can also allow for this kind of distribution, in that the tutor can scaffold the tutee's understanding."[57]

David Boud, Ruth Cohen and Jane Samson, in accordance with this principle, said that:

> "Students learn a great deal by explaining their ideas to others and by participating in activities in which they can learn from their peers."[58]

Distributed cognition makes the learning environment not only productive – due to its collective nature – but also psychologically edifying. Robert E. Slavin wrote: "Similarly, Piaget (1926) held that social-arbitrary

57 Ibid., p. 221.
58 D. Boud, R. Cohen, and J. Sampson, Eds., *Peer Learning in Higher Education: Learning from & with each other* (Virginia: Stylus Publishing Inc., 2001), p. 3.

knowledge – language, values, rules, morality, and symbol systems (such as reading and math) – can be learned only in interactions with others. [...]."[59]

Lillard has pointed out that "Supporting the idea that distributed cognition underlies the benefits of collaborative learning, studies show that transactive dialogues are essential to successful collaborative learning arrangements [...]. In such dialogues, children clearly build on each other's ideas, each providing a bit of scaffolding for the next idea that comes along. [...]."[60]

Working together, students will surely see relations between elements of their understanding in a subject[61] or in the connectedness of life in general.

59 R. E. Slavin, *COOPERATIVE LEARNING: Theory, Research, and Practice* (Boston: Allyn and Bacon, 1995), p. 17.
60 Lillard, p. 221.
61 Michael Prosser and Keith Trigwell, *Understanding Learning and Teaching The Experience in Higher Education* (Philadelphia: The Society for Research into Higher Education and Open University Press, 1999), p. 4.

3.3 ACTIVE LEARNING

Angeline Lillard sustains that "When one moves with a purpose, there is a sense in which one's body is aligned with one's thought. Thought guides action. Thought and body movement can be aligned in other ways as well, as when one moves through represented space or nods one's head while thinking positive thoughts."[62]

Active learning enhances the development of thinking and reasoning in children, a cognitive faculty needed for human survival. As Merril Harmin and Melanie Toth have pointed out:

"[...]. We do not want students asking us every little question that comes to mind. Rather, we want them to think for themselves, managing themselves as intelligently as they can. This is what they, too, want. They do not want to be bossed."[63]

Children actively learn from each other.

---

62 Ibid., p. 51.

63 M. Harmin and M. Toth , *Inspiring Active Learning: A Complete Handbook for Today's Teachers* (Virginia: Association for Supervision and Curriculum Development, 2006), p. 7.

Although one is a little bit advanced than the other (which is expected in peer learning), both develop that interdependence as they harness their ability to think and reason out together (given that they are within their proper age gap). Lillard explained this further: "[…] For Piaget, if the peer's thought processes are too advanced, the tutee cannot accommodate his mental structures to fit the new information. Likewise, if the peer is operating above the tutee's zone of proximal development, the tutee cannot adopt the new reasoning or behavior.[...].”[64]

One study conducted by Maggi Savin-Baden and Claire Howell Major on problem-based learning (PBL), an approach where students learn thinking strategies and domain knowledge, shows how this principle is applied:

> "In our analysis of problem-based learning and the changes it has undergone over time, we argue that flexibility and diversity are vital to ensure that through problem-based learning both students and tutors come to own and value their shifts and

---

64 Lillard, pp. 206-207.

transitions in learning."[65]

Lillard says that "Providing explanations is an active process and is known to improve learning [...]. Children are clearly more active when they learn with peers. In one study, tutees asked 240 times more questions when being tutored by a peer than during whole-class learning with an adult teacher [...]. As compared to passively listening to teachers, as typically occurs in whole-class learning environments in the United States, children appear to more actively contribute to their own education in collaborative and peer tutoring situations."[66]

The relationship between cognition and movement has been well established in scientific research; however, it is almost a pity that, as Maria Montessori indicated, "We have been used to thinking that movement in education, understood to be just a mental relaxation, has been introduced and become mandatory in schools only at a later time in our

65 M. Savin-Badeni and C. H. Major, *Foundations of Problem-based Learning* (England: Open University Press, 2004), p. 3.
66 Lillard, p. 222.

history [...]"[67]

3.4 COGNITION AND MOTIVATION

A child learning from another child embodies with it that deep sense of being inspired and motivated. Paul R. Pintrich and his colleagues stated that: "The relationship between cognition and motivation is an issue that is receiving increased attention in both education and psychology [...]. This attention is the result of an interest on the part of theorists and researchers to understand the combined influences of motivation and cognition on self-directed behavior."[68]

Lillard's statement couldn't be more apt for this purpose: "It goes without saying that when engaged in peer learning, children are involved with each other. This involvement

---

67 Augusto Scocchera (a cura di), *Maria Montessori: Il metodo del bambino e la formazione dell'uomo*. (Roma: Edizione Opera Nazionale Montessori, 2002), p. 48. Translation was done by this author.
68 Paul R. Pintrich, Donald R. Brown, et al., *Student Motivation, Cognition, and Learning: Essays in Honor of Wilbert J. McKeachie* (New Jersey: Lawrence Erlbaum Associates, Inc., 1994), p. 135.

probably motivates learning, as suggested by the studies showing high levels of student satisfaction with peer learning situations. Throughout elementary and high school, social life is increasingly important to children [...]."[69]

The role that a tutor in learning plays on developing the cognitive aspect of a tutee (and vice versa) is paramount for, as David Boud and his colleagues said, "Learning from each other is not only a feature of informal learning, it occurs in all courses at all levels. Students have conversations about what they are learning inside and outside classrooms whether teachers are aware of it or not. The first approach, when stuck on a problem, is normally to ask another student, not the teacher. Not only can they provide each other with useful information but sharing the experience of learning also makes it less burdensome and more enjoyable."[70]

Motivation is key to any form of enjoyable learning. Learning anything devoid of any motivation may be called a forced learning (as

---

69 Lillard, p. 222.
70 D. Boud, et al., p. 1.

schools around the world today have been doing since time immemorial). Lillard noted: "Traditional schools separate children during the learning process, in the sense that children are not supposed to talk to or interact with each other during class. Children try desperately to interact during lecture time in school, passing notes, whispering, and winking, but they usually must wait for recess, lunch, and after school to openly engage in the social interaction that is apparently so desirable."[71]

When traditional schools don't motivate children the way they are handled now – not obviously because of the quality of teachers, but because the system itself doesn't allow it to take place – approaches like peer learning could serve as one of the best solutions. Kofi Marfo and his colleagues have pointed out that: "Over the past two decades, developments occurring contemporaneously in the fields of education and psychology have culminated in substantial intensification of the cognitive education movement. In the field of education, growing discontent – both within and outside the

---

71 Ibid., 222.

education community – about the progressive decline in educational outcomes has resulted in a constant search not only for improved instruction techniques but also for alternative approaches to selecting and defining the content of instruction."[72]

---

72 Robert F. Mulcahy , Robert H. Short, et al., *Enhancing Learning and Thinking.* In Kofi Marfo, Robert F. Mulcahy, David Peat, Jac Andrews and Seokee Cho, *Teaching Cognitive Strategies in the Classroom: A Content-Based Instructional Model* (New York: Praeger Publishers, 1991), p. 67.

4 SOCIAL ASPECTS OF PEER LEARNING

Learning, as we have seen through the lenses of the previous chapters, is best expressed by the presences of both the tutor and the tutee. The social aspects of this form of educative endeavor will be equally important to understand. Diane M. Hogan and her colleagues – discussing the role of Vygotsky's theory to start with – explained it in their own terms:

> "In what ways is Vygotsky's theory relevant to a discussion of collaborative peer learning? Vygotsky's theory views human development as a sociogenetic process by which children gain mastery over cultural tools and signs in the course of interacting with others in their environments. These others are often more competent and help children to understand and use in appropriate ways the tools and signs that are important in the cultural group into which they have been born. This process of interaction between the child and a more competent other is said to effect

development if the interaction occurs within the child's zone of proximal development."[73]

The role of social interaction in the development of cognition has been established to be vital. As Angeliki Nicolopoulou and Michael Cole have pointed out: "One of the most central and distinctive principles of the Vygotskian perspective is that the formation of mind is essentially and inescapably a sociocultural process; consequently, it can be grasped only by situating individual development in its sociocultural context. However, as various scholars have recently pointed out – including the editors of this volume, as well as Wertch (1985), Goodnow (1990), and Nicolopoulou (1991, 1993) – a great deal of the research that has associated itself with the ideas of Vygotsky has focused only on certain limited aspects of the social embeddedness of thought and intellectual development. In particular, with a few exceptions – among which we include some

---

73   Angela M. O'Donnell, and Alison King, Eds., *Cognitive Perspective on Peer Learning*. In Diane M. Hogan and Jonathan R. H. Tudge, *Implications of Vygotsky's Theory for Peer Learning* (p.39). (New Jersey: Lawrence Erlbaum Associates, Inc., 1999), p. 39.

of our own earlier work [...] – it has tended to conceive of the "social" or interpsychological context of development exclusively in terms of face-to-face interaction in dyadic pairs (or, rarely, in small groups)."[74]

It is understood that social factors contributing to cognitive development in children are evidently undeniable in the face of evidence. Luis C. Moll and Kathryn F. Whitmore, in their article, *Vygotsky in Classroom Practice: Moving from Individual Transmission to Social Transaction*, said:

> "Hence he viewed thinking not as a characteristic of the child only, but of the child-in-social-activities with others [...]. In terms of classroom learning, Vygotsky specifically emphasized the relation between thinking and what we would call the social organization of instruction [...]."[75]

---

74 Ellice A. Forman, et al., *Contexts for Learning: Sociocultural Dynamics in Children's Development,* In Angeliki Nicolopoulou and Michael Cole, *Generation and Transmission of Shared Knowledge in the Culture of Collaborative Learning: The Fifth Dimension, Its Play-World, and Its Institutional Contexts* (p.283). (New York: Oxford University Press., 1993), p. 283.
75 Ibid., p. 19.

Although not limited to this number, three aspects of peer learning can be treated in this context: *promotive interaction, social skills, and positive interdependence.*[76]

4.1 PROMOTIVE INTERACTION

The essence of this aspect of learning lies in its facilitative nature in fostering interaction, where the end goal is to achieve productivity.[77] In their *Implications of Piagetian Theory for*

---

76 D.W. Johnson, R.T. Johnson & K.A. Smith, *Active learning: Cooperation in the college classroom* (Minnesota: Interaction Book Company: 1998), https://ows.edb. utexas.edu. The author borrowed the diagram of Johnson, et al (1998) where the actual design can be found on page 5:5 of his book. The three terms appeared in an article entitled "Social Aspects of Learning and CSCL" from the site: https://ows.edb.-utexas.edu where OWS is a service provided to faculty and students in the College of Education at The University of Texas at Austin. The author uses the three terms in the context of peer learning as opposed to the context of cooperation as conveyed in the book by the aforementioned authors. The triangle is as follows: Promotive Interaction (Achievement Productivity as goal); Social Skills and Group Processing (Psychological Health); Positive Interdependence (Positive Relationships). CSCL stands for Computer-supported collaborative learning. However, this author develops his own definitions from these three terms. Site access date: June 26, 2016.

77 Ibid. This is a personally modified definition. Johnson and his colleagues define it as "when the members of the learning team or community actively encourage, support and facilitate each other's efforts to complete tasks and responsibilities to achieve the group's goals." The diagram has in it achievement productivity as the goal of promotive interaction.

Peer Learning, De Lisi and Golbeck wrote: "A second reason for the current popularity of peer learning derives from the fundamental task that schools face in preparing students for life after school in the workplace and in communities. Classroom-based peer learning activities are considered an important aspect of preparation for life after formal schooling ends. Learning how to work together cooperatively is a valued educational activity derived from the larger cultural context in which schools exist."[78]

Interaction between two children at an early age can indeed be a valid formula for future success in life. What it promotes is children's ability to see and understand how being with another human being (as either with the tutor or with the tutee) can be life's daily reality. William Damon wrote:

> "[...] Research has shown that peer learning can bolster children's self'-esteem, awaken their interest in challenging tasks, enhance scholarly achievement, and foster prosocial behavior. [..]."[79]

---

78 Angela O'Donnell, et al., p. 4.
79 Damon, p. 331

Exposing a child at a young age with the task of working with another child slightly younger or older than herself or himself can bolster prosocial behavior because of the nature of experience it can offer both (parents whose children go to traditional schools register their kids in some extracurricular activity like the YMCA to have this interaction)[80]. In *Classroom Interaction and Social Learning*, Kumpulainen and Wray said that "Specific attention was paid to the purposes for which the students used their oral language in collaborative interactions with their peers and how these interactions reflected their writing and learning processes. The data collection for this study was undertaken through two case studies conducted with primary-aged students. The themes of students' writing ranged from narrative texts to informative texts. The findings of this study show that the students' verbal interactions in the social contexts created by the use of word processors were highly task related, characterised by the exchange of information,

---

80 Patricia A. Adler, and Peter Adler, *Peer Power: Preadolescent Culture and Identity* (New Jersey: Rutgers University Press, 1998), p. 98.

questioning, judging, organising and composing."[81]

In terms of achievement productivity, both children in peer learning can accomplish the task better than when they do the same task independently. Citing the studies done by Willem Doise, William Damon explained:

> "[...] In one critical study, Doise found that children's collective performances were superior to those of group members taken individually both in cases where children were paired with peers more advanced and less advanced than themselves. [...]"[82]

4.2 SOCIAL SKILLS

Peer learning helps develop social skills in children. Social skills, in turn, builds psychological health.[83] Associating a child with

---

81 Kristina Kumpulainen and David Wray, Eds., *Classroom Interaction and Social Learning: From Theory to Practice* (New York: RoutledgeFalmer, 2002), p. 57.

82 Damon, p. 336.

83 Johnson, et al. This part of the triangle (Social Skills and Group Processing), based on their definition, involves the group reflecting on completed task and the progress to 1) describe what members actions were helpful and unhelpful in accomplishing the assignment, and 2) make decisions about what actions to continue or change to be more effective in the future (https://ows.edb.utexas.edu /site/computer-

another child or with a community early in life is beneficial in this development. Annemarie Sullivan Palincsar, Ann L. Brown and Joseph C. Campione in their article, *First-Grade Dialogues for Knowledge Acquisition and Use,* reported: "Increased attention to the dialectical relation between the individual and the social aspects in the acquisition of knowledge has led to a burgeoning of interest regarding collaborative learning. Whether propelled by Piagetian theory regarding the role of cognitive conflict in the presence of differing perspectives or Vygotskian theory regarding the internalization of dialogues initially experienced in social contexts, there is interest in how increasing divergent classrooms can become learning communities – communities in which each participant makes significant contributions to the emergent understandings of all members, despite having unequal knowledge concerning the topic under study."[84]

On a scholastic level, teachers or educators are the ones in charge in making sure

supported-collaborative-learning-2011/6-social-aspects-learning-cscl).
84   Forman, et al., p. 43.

this learning takes place either in a traditional classroom environment or otherwise; however, this need to learn things from each other as a social skill brings with it a new way of how we define teachers in the twenty-first century. As David Boud and his colleagues have pointed out:

> "As teachers, we often fool ourselves in thinking that what we do is necessarily more important for student learning than other activities in which they engage. Our role is vital. However, if we place ourselves in the position of mediating all that students need to know, we not only create unrealistic expectations but we potentially deskill students by preventing them from developing the vital skills of effectively learning from each other needed in life and work."[85]

What a child develops in being able to teach another child (not very much distant from him or her in age) is the psychological thought of social involvement and responsibility as proven, for instance, by the highly regarded results of peer-assisted learning.[86] The tutee,

---

85 Boud, p.2.
86 Keith Topping and Stewart Ehly, Eds.. *Peer-Assisted Learning*. In Herbert J. Walberg, *Foreword* (New Jersey: Lawrence Erlbaum

sensing the presence of another individual with whom she or he can fully communicate, engages in this social activity as naturally as can be expected. As William Damon commented: "Thus, according to Piaget, children gain both social and cognitive benefits from peer interaction. The social benefits are their improved communication skills and their sharper sense of other person's perspectives. The cognitive benefits are the urge to reexamine the truth of one's own conceptions and the guidance of another's feedback in this process. Piaget believed that these social and cognitive benefits were directly related, in that improved social communication instigates progressive cognitive change. When people communicate well with one another, they realize the need to explain and justify their beliefs, which in turn forces them to rationalize their beliefs as much as possible. [...]"[87]

Peer learning should ensure children communicate well with one another. And because of this, it has now become the duty of

Associates, 1998), p. IX.
87 Damon, p. 333.

educators to implement change in accordance with this basic principle of learning, as Dennie Briggs explained:

> "The current push to increase literacy in schools offers an unprecedented opportunity to address a number of pressing social issues simultaneously. In addition to reducing illiteracy, we could revitalize public education as we know it and bring about significant changes in the way children and young people learn. We could change the way teachers instruct. Furthermore, we could modify how older and younger children view each other. And finally, we could bridge the gap between generations leading to a more vital, human existence for us all."[88]

When traditional schools don't foster this basic social need of children – for "Results clearly support the claim that traditional classrooms can have deleterious effects on peer relations, both within and between ethnic groups, even though all pupils tend to like each other more over the course of the academic year"[89]– it is but imperative to welcome and

88 Briggs, p. XV. This is the Introduction to the Book.
89 Shlomo Sharan, Peter Kussell, et al., *COOPERATIVE LEARNING:*

embrace educational methods and systems that really work.

4.3   POSITIVE INTERDEPENDENCE

Peer learning encourages positive interdependence which will build up positive relationships in the long run. To this effect, Shlomo Sharan and his colleagues, their research focusing on desegregated schools, reported: "Research on the effects of cooperative learning [under which peer learning is classified] in the classroom on children's social relations has dealt largely with attitudinal changes and friendship patterns as expressed in sociometric measures. [...] ."[90]

Positive interdependence, a social aspect of peer learning which creates and harnesses relationships between and among children, strengthens the bonding that develops from this

---

Research in Desegregated Schools. (New Jersey: Lawrence Erlbaum Associates, Inc., 1984), p. 131.

90   Ibid., p. 74.

personal contact of children as human beings. The sense of inevitably working together through thick and thin to accomplish an important goal which may benefit and contribute for the betterment of society is a reality that they will begin to fully understand later on in life.

Peer learning facilitates in bridging and strengthening this bonding, as De Lisi and Golbeck have observed:

> "Collaborative work between students has become an important means of implementing constructivist educational approaches. Professional associations such as the International Reading Association, the National Association for the Education of Young Children, and the National Council of Teachers of Mathematics have each endorsed peer learning as a means to enhance the teaching-learning process."[91]

Endorsing peer learning to enhance the learning process and achieve optimal interdependence among children has become a necessary step to a more effective and

91 O'Donnell, et al., p. 4.

efficacious education. Peer learning, however, involves the participation of the educator, the tutor and the tutee to make this whole thing work. Dennie Briggs noted: "Nothing succeeds like success. After peer teacher and student have established a relationship, each should have a satisfying experience. Teaching is best begun in small manageable morsels, bits that can be completed in a single lesson. And then after this initial encounter, the peer teacher can undertake more ambitious tasks. A teacher is available to offer support, but remains unobtrusive during the teaching session."[92]

The relationship between a tutor and the tutee weighs heavier when compared to the relationship between the educator and the tutor. The reason behind lies in the fact that interdependent relationship must be focused on children as they are the ones who would be expected to perform in life in the end. However, the role of a teacher can in no way be disparaged. Briggs commented:

---

92 Briggs, p. 45.

"Following the teaching session, the teacher meets with the peer teachers in a tutorial to review their experience. What went over well and what went wrong? What different ways of teaching could have been more effective? The teacher offers expertise on teaching and observing, and in so doing, forms a new relationship with the peer teachers – that of colleague or mentor. The new role is often in sharp contrast to the authoritarian one of the traditional teacher."[93]

---

93 Ibid.

5 MARIA MONTESSORI'S SOCIO-COGNITIVE APPROACH TO PEER AND COLLABORATIVE LEARNING

Talking of a child, Maria Montessori said: "To grow up and become a man is the child's one great mission which is pushing him."[94] As a matter of fact peer learning, as a method, is effective enough to facilitate that one great mission that pushes the child to grow up as a man. And Montessori's well-founded system of learning is there to ensure that the child's becoming a man will be both meaningful and socio-cognitively constructive. The reason being that Montessori method is life and living itself; it is action that counts, as Angeline Lillard has pointed out:

> "[···] Dr. Montessori repeatedly claimed
> that people learn not by being told, but by

---

94 M. Montessori, *Montessori: La Scoperta del bambino* (Milano: Garzanti Libri S.R.L., 1999), p. 67

watching and by doing. Thus teachers show, rather than tell, children how to engage in the work.[...]"[95]

Work is the key word of Montessori education. For Montessori the senses play an intelligent role in shaping the mind of a child, which are being stimulated through an activity Montessori schools call as working. Gerald Lee Gutek, in his book, *Maria Montessori and the Montessori Method: The Origins of an Educational Innovation*, wrote: "The sense exercises constitute a species of auto-education, which, if these exercises be many times repeated, leads to a perfecting of the child's psycho-sensory processes. The directress must intervene to lead the child from sensations to ideas – from the concrete to the abstract, and to the association of ideas.[...]"[96]

What is evident in Montessori education lies in how peer learning assists in the child's natural ability to observe and imitate his or her partner's activities – and learn from them by

---

95 Lillard. p. 198.
96 Gerald Lee Gutek, Ed., *Maria Montessori and the Montessori Method: The Origins of an Educational Innovation* (New York: Rowman & Littlefield Publishers, Inc., 2004), p. 181.

actually performing the tasks on the spot. Maria Montessori said that "People sometimes fear that if a child of five gives lessons, this will hold him back in his own progress. But, in the first place, he does not teach all the time and his freedom is respected. Second, teaching helps him to understand what he knows even better than before. He has to analyze and rearrange his little store of knowledge before he can pass it on."[97]

Maria Montessori said these words with an authority of an educator – someone who could read events and developments way, way ahead into the future. As G. L. Gutek explained:

> "[…] Montessori's method of education was based on her conception of science, on her observations of children, and on her extensive research in anthropology, psychology, and pedagogy. From research and experience, she arrived at a series of "discoveries," or assumptions, about children's growth, development, and education.[...] "[98]

97 Lillard, p. 209.
98 Gutek, p. 45.

5.1   INTELLECTUAL EDUCATION[99]

In a Montessori school environment, children are always busy doing something. The environment causes the children's movements and activities; it prompts them to do an activity that meets and excites their curiosity. Gutek wrote:

> "For Montessori, the educative process embraced two key and necessary elements: the individual child and the environment. The primary element is the individual child's physiological and mental constitution, which gives her or him the power to act. As a real biological entity, the living child has a body, a physiological structure that grows and develops; however, each child also has a spiritual soul, a psychic form that manifests itself. The environment, the secondary element, provides the necessary milieu in which the human being develops. The child's education requires an environment in which he or she can develop the powers given by nature. Education then is a process of

---

99 This sub-chapter title was borrowed by this author from Gerald Lee Gutek's Chapter 15 title of his aforementioned book for the purpose of explaining the cognitive aspect of peer and collaborative learning in Montessori method.

collaboration with the child's nature and stages of development."[100]

Collaborative learning, given a prepared environment which can excite the children's intellect and senses (through the use of well-studied and scientifically proven educative materials), has in itself the function to serve as a natural by-product of Nature, which could lead the children to the serendipitous and mutual uncovering of the many secrets of Mother Nature for "they motivate one another to acquire new knowledge and generate the constructive feedback that enables them to improve their reasoning abilities [...]"[101]

In Montessori terms having a prepared environment entails setting of the classroom and arranging the materials in good order before the children arrive in school (and children are sensitive to order[102]). Specifically, Lillard noted that "Although few materials require collaborative use, most Montessori Elementary materials can easily accommodate

100 Gutek., p. 46.
101 Damon, p. 338.
102 Maria Montessori, *Montessori: Il segreto dell'infanzia*. (Milano: Garzanti Libri S.p.a., 1999), p. 67.

two or more users. The Grammar Box Command Cards are an example of a work that can be done with others or alone. Children pick up a card and read its message, which (for a verb card) might be "Waddle across the room like a duck." To use these cards collaboratively, others guess what command is being enacted. Montessori teachers say that the cards seem to increase inspiration for reading among younger children; for all children, they help make clear the parts of speech."[103]

Since peer or collaborative learning happens all the time in Montessori schools, educators are left to observe and help those children who are really in need of them – which, in this case, basically gives the educator ample time to carry out. To see how a real and actual scenario works in a Montessori classroom environment, Gerald Gutek's own observation can be worthwhile for this purpose:

> "One day, when I entered one of the "Children's Houses," five or six little ones gathered quietly about me and began caressing, lightly, my hands, and my clothing,

103 Lillard, p. 217.

saying, "It is smooth." "It is velvet." "This is rough." A number of others came near and began with serious and intent faces to repeat the same words, touching me as they did so. The directress wished to interfere to release me, but I signed to her to be quiet, and I myself did not move, but remained silent, admiring this spontaneous intellectual activity of my little ones. The greatest triumph of our educational method should always be this: *to bring about the spontaneous progress of the child.*"[104]

What this observation teaches, among other things, is that children need not be taught what to learn for they themselves – offered with the opportunity set by the environment and the occasion to decipher it – would, as a group, voluntarily seek for the knowledge and information it can naturally provide them.

---

104 Gutek, p. 183. It is very important to understand how Montessori schools educate children using the Montessori Method. On page 182, Gutek explained: "So, for example, touching the smooth and rough cards in the first tactile exercise, she [the educator] should say, "This is smooth," repeating the words with varying modulations of the voice, always letting the tones be clear and the enunciation very distinct. "Smooth, smooth, smooth. Rough, rough, rough." In the same way, when treating of the sensations of heat and cold, she must say, "This is cold." "This is hot." "This is ice-cold." "This is tepid" She may then begin to use the generic terms, "heat," "more heat," "less heat," and so forth."

Lillard further explained that "When schools use collaborative learning or peer tutoring programs, they are usually instituted as a special program, something children do for an hour each week or perhaps each day. Even such limited exposure has benefits. However, as the psychologist Barbara Rogoff and her colleagues describe (and it bears repeating), "adding the technique" of having children work in cooperative learning teams is quite different than a system in which collaboration is inherent in the structure."[105]

While traditional schools apply peer learning methods as an additional strategy to education, Montessori schools apply them as the central teaching methodology. One highly regarded socio-cognitive approach to peer and collaborative learning in a Montessori classroom setting is the spontaneous and dynamic interaction with a prepared environment while working together as a group of two or more. Lillard explained one specific scenario to demonstrate how it is done by way of one of the Montessori activities in a classroom: "The Bank

105 Lillard, p. 223.

Game is an Elementary material designed specifically for group use, particularly to work on multiplication. The materials for the Bank Game are set of the same arabic numeral cards used with many other Montessori math materials, such as the Golden Beads, a second set of gray number cards, which serve as the multiplier, and a third set of cards, which are used to indicate the product. These last cards can indicate numbers up to 9 million."[106]

The activity just mentioned fosters collaboration on a socio-cognitive level and Montessori methods allow this to happen practically every single day. Gerald Gutek stresses that:

---

[106] Ibid., p. 216. Lillard, explaining the mechanism of this activity, continued: "Three children, usually around 9 years old, take roles: one child plays the Banker, the second, the Teller, and the third, the Customer. The role of the teller is more communicative than substantial, and thus the teller can be a younger child whose mathematical knowledge is less advanced: he or she will learn by watching the customer and the banker. The customer may say to the teller, "I want 8,642 multiplied by 34." The children then decompose the multiplicand into its categorical part (thousands, hundreds. And so on), and then do the same for the multiplier. They lay out cards showing the problem and begin their series of multiplications category by category. The tell then gives the banker the first transaction: "I would like to have the product of 4 x 2, please ." The banker offers the customer the card for 8 units.[...]."

"Our educational aim with very young children must be to aid the spontaneous development of the mental, spiritual, and physical personality, and not to make of the child a cultured individual in the commonly accepted sense of the term. So, after we have offered to the child such didactic material as is adapted to provoke the development of his senses, we must wait until the activity known as observation develops. And herein lies the art of the educator; in knowing how to measure the action by which we help the young child's personality to develop. To one whose attitude is right, little children soon reveal profound individual differences which call for very different kinds of help from the teacher. Some of them require almost no intervention on her part, while others demand actual teaching. It is necessary, therefore, that the teaching shall be rigorously guided by the principle of limiting to the greatest possible point the active intervention of the educator."[107]

107 Gutek, pp. 184-185.

5.2   LEARNING SOCIAL BEHAVIOR IN MONTESSORI

Another socio-cognitive approach to peer and collaborative learning of the Montessori method is the art of working together to develop social behavior. Angeline Lillard's statement on this sets the context: "Another aspect of Montessori education that is learned in part via observation and imitation is social behavior. Montessori education includes explicit instruction on social behavior in a part of the curriculum called the lessons of Grace and Courtesy, which are on a par with lessons in math, music, and language. The goal of Montessori education, in fact, is explicitly stated to be the education of the whole person, not only the intellect."[108]

Both the intellect and the social behavior have been given equal status in a Montessori education. The development of social behavior, however, must come as a natural consequence to

_____
108 Lillard, pp. 198-199.

a set of conduct understood by a child to be proper and good. Lillard explained:

"Unlike other lessons, the lessons of Grace and Courtesy are often shown to the entire class at once, perhaps because gracious social behavior is so clearly a community endeavor. In the lessons of Grace and Courtesy, Primary children are shown how to quietly push in a chair, how to walk alongside someone's rug without knocking over their work, how to make a polite request, how to serve food, and so on. Dr. Montessori even gave children lessons on how to blow their noses, something adults routinely do but rarely stop to teach [...]"[109]

---

109 Ibid. Lillard, on page 199, elaborated this lesson as she said: "At older ages, for the lessons of Grace and Courtesy, children might be asked to act out social scenarios for the class, demonstrating successful and unsuccessful ways to interact with others. Acting out in front of the class specific behaviors and how to respond provides children with practice in the good behaviors, as well as opportunities to observe such behaviors (good and bad) in others. Elementary Montessori teachers say that children of these ages find acting out bad behaviors (either by the teacher pretending to be a child, or by another child) hilariously funny, and that this makes it a particularly effective way to teach. Children can then imitate the good behaviors and should know not to imitate the bad ones. Given the research just described, it would be interesting to know whether this is fully successful or if simply acting out the bad behaviors leads children to be somewhat more apt to be rude. Perhaps watching a rude example that is explicitly designated as rude enables children to inhibit copying it."

The central responsibility of educators lies in making sure children are not only educated on the level of the brain (like most traditional teachers do), but cultivating this sacred and social aspect of human education as well. The Montessori method has indeed been complying with this basic rule through their informed educators for more than half a century. Carlen Henington and Christopher H. Skinner in their article, *Peer Monitoring,* have pointed this out succinctly: "In our society, more is being demanded from educators. Teachers are expected to teach, improve, and maintain appropriate social and academic skills and to decrease, eliminate, and prevent inappropriate social and academic behaviors."[110]

Social and academic skills are both needed by children for them to cope with the demands of living. Social skills in Montessori are developed by way of modeling. Lillard, elaborating on this, has pointed out that

---

110 Keith Topping and Stewart Ehly, Eds., *Peer-Assisted Learning,* In Carlen Henington and Christopher H. Skinner, *Peer Monitoring* (New Jersey: Lawrence Erlbaum Associates, 1998), p. 237.

"Teachers tell stories of heroes and heroines, with the aim of inspiring children to perform heroic deeds in their turn. This practice better aligns with the research showing that merely entertaining particular concepts leads to behaving analogously. The Montessori curriculum explicitly uses modeling and stories to teach social behavior."[111]

One important aspect of Montessori method is the concept that competition is ineffective. Dr. Montessori has understood early on the negative effect of competition in the growth of a child.[112] Cooperation is better than competition. Shlomo Sharan and his colleagues, who authored the book, *Cooperative Learning: Research in Desegregated Schools*, gave this observation:

> "However, we wish to emphasize that even children who are allegedly "competitive" in orientation adapt positively to cooperative modes of interaction with classmates when classroom structure and

111 Lillard, p. 199.
112 "Is Montessori Opposed to Competition?" Pioneer Valley Montessori School (PVMS),http://pvms.org/ about/faq1/ismontessorioppose2/ (June 29, 2016).

social norms facilitate and support cooperation. Children who participated in cooperative small-group learning said they preferred cooperative to competitive relations with classmates [...]."[113]

When the environment supports cooperation, children prefer this model more than anything else. Montessori classrooms support collaborative efforts (cooperation is a specific kind of collaboration[114]) where children work together as friends instead of competitors. Robert E. Slavin in his book, *COOPERATIVE LEARNING: Theory, Research, and Practice,* said: "There are many reasons that cooperative learning is entering the mainstream of educational practice. One is the extraordinary research base [...] supporting the use of cooperative learning to increase student achievement, as well as such other outcomes as improved intergroup relations, acceptance of academically handicapped class-

---

113 S. Sharan, et. al., p. 75.

114 "What are cooperative and collaborative learning?" WNET EDUCATION, http://www.thirteen.org/edonline/concept2class/coopcollab/.Collaborative learning is defined here as a method of teaching and learning in which students team together to explore a significant question or create a meaningful project; whereas, cooperative learning is defined as a specific kind of collaborative learning.

mates, and increased self-esteem. Another reason is the growing realization that students need to learn to think, to solve problems, and to integrate and apply knowledge and skills, and that cooperative learning is an excellent means to that end."[115]

What current research is favoring as a pedagogical method would redound to the approach Montessori schools use across the globe, and one in which Dr. Montessori stands out as one of the most valued educators of all time. Raniero Regni, in his book, *Infanzia e società in Maria Montessori. Il bambino padre dell'uomo*, stated that: "Her [method] is present in time without having to follow its trend. To follow Montessori is to fulfill what Schiller has advised: live in you century without being its creature [inhabitant]; provide what your contemporaries are in need of, not that which they want. Great authors are aware of their epoch and are not paying attention to its trend. And this is the case of Montessori. She is herself

---

115 Slavin, p. 2.

in her time without being caught up with it. Though looking at it on top of a great theory, she is being present in reality, at the heart of her time without being lost in its irreducible diversity. Montessori is capable of handing back the [systems of] education of our [present] time at a time that is ours."[116]

---

116 R. Regni, *Infanzia e società in Maria Montessori. Il bambino padre dell'uomo* (Roma: Armando, 2007), p. 10.

CONCLUSION

Before giving a summary of the main arguments this author has discussed in the body of this work, it is fitting – for the sake of formality – to recall the central concept with which this scholastic endeavor has begun. The central argument of this author has been the following inquiry: What is the role of Maria Montessori in educating the children of this generation and beyond? Specifically, based on scientific evidence, what are the cognitive and social aspects of peer learning as embodied in Maria Montessori's approach to education?

The historical context in which this issue came into being – taking into account educators from the 19th all the way through the 21st century – would have to be traced back in time. What brings the discussion on effective and efficacious education back to life again – inside school boardrooms and offices of Ministers of Education from around the globe – is the fact that the present education (as I have pointed out in the introduction) has been a failure. Giving a brief overview of what happened, Kofi Marfo and his colleagues gave this statement:

> "The forces shaping the discontent with educational outcomes all over the world often have their origins in broader concerns of a socio-politico-economic nature. For example, the politics of technological advancements in space travel, touched off by the launching of Sputnik by the Soviets, was a critical factor in the emergence of the cognitive movement in education in North America during the early 1960s. American educators began to turn away from behaviorism and toward cognitivism in their search for alternative methods and contents of instruction to produce generations of thinkers and problem solvers capable of launching America competitively into the space age."[117]

---

117 Rober F. Mulcahy, et al., p.67.

The socio-politico-economic nature of this issue which has brought the educational system to a total failure could be seen as a turning point from which humanity has to move on. Although there is no single answer to better education in general,[118] the present system of education – in favor of a brighter future of today's children – must not be carried on to the next generation. The Montessori method presents itself as the best known alternative to the collapsing system of traditional schooling. We all want to educate children the best way, especially the poor and the needy. Helen Abadzi in her report, for instance, remarked: "Educating the poor is a large-scale effort in which the World Bank and the donor community have focused since the 1980s. Its apex has been the Education for All (EFA) initiative that promotes primary school completion for all children by 2015. EFA supports achievement of the Millennium Development Goals that aim at reducing poverty by improving the planet's human capital

118 Nicholas C. Polos, *The Dynamics of Team Teaching* (Iowa: Wm. C. Brown Company Publishers, 1965), p. 6.

and resources."[119]

The central theme of this study deals with the efficacy and effectiveness of peer learning (understood here in terms of its collaborative and cooperative nature) in the context of Montessori's approach to education. The scientific findings of Angeline Lillard have been in favor of this position, as Shlomo Sharan, to this effect, further testifies that:

> "Research and development on cooperative learning methods and their effects on pupils in classrooms has its roots in work done decades ago. Nevertheless, systematic research in substantial quantity and with the required degree of controls and sophistication has been published only during the past 15 years. Within this relatively short period of time, cooperative learning underwent a renaissance and has generated considerable interest among educators responsible for the daily work of instruction, as well as among researchers concerned with a wide range of educational, psychological, and social issues. Foremost among these

---

119 H. Abadzi, (2006), *Efficient Learning for the Poor: Insights from the Frontier of Cognitive Neuroscience* (U.S.A.: Office of the Publisher, The World Bank, 2006), p. 4.

issues are the improvement of student academic achievement and promotion of high-level thinking as well as positive interpersonal and inter-group relations among students in school."[120]

As a short response to the main argument of the book, it will therefore be confidently safe and reasonable to state that cognitive and social aspects to peer learning and Dr. Maria Montessori's educative approach to education have scientific grounds. Robyn Gillies declares that "There is no doubt that the benefits attributed to cooperative learning are widespread and numerous. Moreover, it is the apparent success of this approach to learning that led Slavin (1999) to propose that it is one of the greatest educational innovations of recent times."[121]

In honor of her great contribution to the present study and the study of Montessori and her method in general, this author, as a final note, would like to leave the following words of

120 Sharan, p. 285.
121 Gillies, Robyn M. .Cooperative Learning: Integrating Theory and Practice (Los Angeles: Sage Publications, 2007), p. 1.

Angeline Stoll Lillard as a concluding statement:

"It is this practical approach that explains why Dr. Montessori is less debunkable today than Piaget. Like Dr. Montessori, Jean Piaget made many brilliant observations of children, based on their interactions with stimuli he developed. Piaget's aim through these observations was to explain the ontogenesis of intelligence, but for him theory came early, leaving him vulnerable to making observations that fit his theory. Dr. Montessori's aim was instead practical: she sought to develop a system of education that worked with children, rather than against them. Dr. Montessori was not particularly interested in theory; she was a physician, concerned with treatments to aid health and well-being. Surely her personal view did sometimes get in the way of objective observation, but her major ideas about treatments that bring about more optimal learning and development, based on her empirical observations, are largely upheld by research today. If schooling were evidence-based, I think all schools would look a lot more like Montessori schools. Yet Montessori schooling can often feel uncomfortable to parents, and even to the teachers who employ the methods, because it is different from what we had as children. For psychology researchers, attitudes toward Montessori are mixed: some know enough to appreciate it, others misunderstood a small aspect and dismiss the entire approach. Very few know more than a smidgen about it."[122]

---

122 Lillard, p. viii. This is the Preface to her book.

BIBLIOGRAPHY

Abadzi, Helen. *Efficient Learning for the Poor: Insights from the Frontier of Cognitive Neuroscience.* U.S.A.: Office of the Publisher, The World Bank, 2006.

Adler, Patricia A., and Adler, Peter. *Peer Power: Preadolescent Culture and Identity.* New Jersey: Rutgers University Press, 1998.

Biggs, John. *Teaching for Quality Learning at University: What the Student Does.* United Kingdom: McGraw-Hill House, 2003.

Boud, David, Cohen Ruth, and Sampson, Jane. Eds. *Peer Learning in Higher Education: Learning from & with each other.* Virginia: Stylus Publishing Inc, 2001.

Briggs, Dennie. *A Class of Their Own: When Children Teach Children.* Connecticut: Greenwood Publishing Group, 1998.

Damon, William and Phelps, Erin. *"CRITICAL DISTINCTIONS AMONG THREE APPROACHES TO PEER EDUCATION."* Journal of Applied Developmental Psychology. Volume 13. 1989.

Damon, William, *"Peer Education: The Untapped Potential."* Journal of Applied Developmental Psychology 5 October 1984.

Falchikov, Nancy. *Learning Together: Peer Tutoring in Higher Education.* London: RoutledgeFalmer, 2001.

Forman, Ellice A., et al. *Contexts for Learning: Sociocultural Dynamics in Children's Development.* New York: Oxford University Press, 1993.

Frank, Ivan C. *Building Self-Esteem in At-Risk Youth: Peer Group Programs and Individual Success Stories.* Connecticut: Praeger Westport, 1996.

Gillies, Robyn M. *Cooperative Learning: Integrating Theory and Practice.* Los Angeles: Sage Publications, 2007.

Grazzini, Camillo. *Studi Montessori: I Quattro Piani dello Sviluppo,"* Il Quaderno Montessori, Anno XIII, numero 51 (Autunno 1996).

Guilmette, J-H. *ower of peer learning : networks and development P cooperation.* Canada: International

Development Research Center, 2009.

Gutek, Gerald Lee. Ed. *Maria Montessori and the Montessori Method: The Origins of an Educational Innovation.* New York: Rowman & Littlefield Publishers, Inc., 2004.

Harmin, Merril, Toth Melanie. *Inspiring Active Learning: A Complete Handbook for Today's Teachers.* Virginia: Association for Supervision and Curriculum Development, 2006.

Hurault, Bernardo. Ed. *Christian Community Bible.* China: Nanjing Amity Pinting Company, 2003.

Johnson, D.W., Johnson, R.T. & Smith, K.A. *Active learning: Cooperation in the college classroom.* Minnesota: Interaction Book Company, 1998.

Jones, Kevin and Charlton, Tony. Eds. *Overcoming Learning and Behaviour Difficulties: Partnership with Pupils.* New York: Routledge, 1996.

Kumpulainen, Kristina and Wray, David. Eds. *Classroom Interaction and Social Learning: From Theory to Practice.* New York: RoutledgeFalmer, 2002.

Lillard, Angeline Stoll. *Montessori: The Science Behind The Genius (New York: Oxford University Press, 2005.*

Montessori, Maria. *Montessori: La Scoperta del bambino.* Milano: Garzanti Libri S.R.L., 1999.

Montessori, Maria. *Montessori: Il segreto dell'infanzia*. Milano: Garzanti Libri S.p.a., 1999.

Moyles, Janet R. *Organizing for Learning in the Primary Classroom: A Balanced Approach to Classroom Management*. Philadelphia: Open University Press, 1992.

Mulcahy, Robert F., Short, Robert H., et al. *Enhancing Learning and Thinking*. New York: Praeger Publishers, 1991.

O'Donnell, Angela M. and King, Alison. Eds. *Cognitive Perspective on Peer Learning*. New Jersey: Lawrence Erlbaum Associates, Inc., 1999.

Pintrich, Paul R., Brown, Donald R., et al. *Student Motivation, Cognition, and Learning: Essays in Honor of Wilbert J. McKeachie*. New Jersey: Lawrence Erlbaum Associates, Inc, 1994.

Polos, Nicholas C. *The Dynamics of Team Teaching*. Iowa: Wm. C. Brown Company Publishers, 1965.

Prosser, Michael and Trigwell, Keith. *Understanding Learning and Teaching The Experience in Higher Education,* Philadelphia: The Society for Research into Higher Education and Open University Press, 1999.

Psotka, Joseph, Massey, Dan L., et al. *Intelligent Tutoring Systems: Lessons Learned*. New Jersey: Lawrence Erlbaum Associates Publishers, 1988.

Regni, Raniero. *Infanzia e società in Maria Montessori. Il bambino padre dell'uomo*. Roma: Armando, 2007.

Robbins, Pam. *Peer Coaching: To Enrich Professional Practice, School Culture, and Student Learning*. Virginia: ASCD, 2015.

Robinson, K. *Ken Robinson: How to escape education's death valley* [Video file]. May 28, 2013. Retrievedfrom(https://www.youtube.com/watch?v=wX78iKhInsc).

Savin-Baden, Maggi and Major, Claire Howell. *Foundations of Problem-based Learning*. England: Open University Press, 2004.

Scocchera, Augusto (a cura di). *Maria Montessori: Il metodo del bambino e la formazione dell'uomo*. Roma: Edizione Opera Nazionale Montessori, 2002.

Segal, Judith W., et al. (Eds.). *Thinking and Learning Skills: Relating Instruction to Research*. Vol.1. New Jersey: Lawrence Erbaum Associates, Inc, 1985.

Sharan, Shlomo (Ed.) *COOPERATIVE LEARNING: Theory and Research*. Connecticut London: Praeger Westport, 1990.

Sharan, Shlomo, et al. *COOPERATIVE LEARNING IN THE CLASSROOM: Research in Desegregated Schools*. New Jersey: Lawrence Erlbaum Associates, Publishers, 1984.

Slavin, Robert E. *COOPERATIVE LEARNING: Theory, Research, and Practice.* Boston: Allyn and Bacon, 1995.

"Social Aspect of Learning & CSCL." OWS. University of Texas. Austin. June 20, 2016 (https://ows.edb.utexas.edu/site/computer/supported-collaborative-learning-2011/6-social-aspects-learning-cscl).

Speece, Deborah L. and Keogh, Barbara K. (Eds) (1996). *Research on Classroom Ecologies: Implications for Inclusion of Children With Learning Disabilities.* New Jersey: Lawrence Erlbaum Associates, Publishers.

Topping, Keith and Ehly, Stewart. Eds. *Peer-Assisted Learning.* New Jersey: Lawrence Erlbaum Associates, 1998.

Torff, Bruce and Sternberg, Robert J.Eds. *Understanding and Teaching the Intuitive Mind: Student and Teacher Learning.* New Jersey: Lawrence Erlbaum Associates, Publishers, 2001.

Trabalzini, Paola (a cura di). "*Maria Montessori Diario di una scienziata: imparare osservando.*" VITA DELL'INFANZIA Anno LXIII, N. 2. Settembre/Ottobre, 2014.

Wong, Bernie Y.L. and Donahue, Mavis L. Eds. *The Social Dimensions of Learning Disabilities: Essays in Honor of Tanis Bryan.* New Jersey: Lawrence Erlbaum Associates, Publishers, 2002.

Author index

Subject index